Famou

Siege of Yorktown

Renato Frost

Alpha Editions

Contents

Introduction

The Siege of Yorktown, ending on October 19, 1781, at Yorktown, Virginia, was a decisive victory by a combined force of American Continental Army troops led by General George Washington and French Army troops led by the Comte de Rochambeau over a British Army commanded by British peer and Lieutenant General Charles Cornwallis. The culmination of the Yorktown campaign, the siege proved to be the last major land battle of the American Revolutionary War in the North American theater, as the surrender by Cornwallis, and the capture of both him and his army, prompted the British government to negotiate an end to the conflict. The battle boosted faltering American morale and revived French enthusiasm for the war, as well as undermining popular support for the conflict in Great Britain.

In 1780, approximately 5,500 French soldiers landed in Rhode Island to assist their American allies in operations against British-controlled New York City. Following the arrival of dispatches from France that included the possibility of support from the French West Indies fleet of the Comte de Grasse, Washington and Rochambeau decided to ask de Grasse for assistance either in besieging New York, or in military operations against a British army operating in Virginia. On the advice of Rochambeau, de Grasse informed them of his intent to sail to the Chesapeake Bay, where Cornwallis had taken command of the army. Cornwallis, at first given confusing orders by his superior officer, Henry Clinton, was eventually ordered to build a defensible deep-water port, which he began to do in Yorktown, Virginia. Cornwallis' movements in Virginia were shadowed by a Continental Army force led by the Marquis de Lafayette.

The French and American armies united north of New York City during the summer of 1781. When word of de Grasse's decision arrived, both armies began moving south toward Virginia, engaging in tactics of deception to lead the British to believe a siege of New York was planned. De Grasse sailed from the West Indies and arrived at the Chesapeake Bay at the end of August, bringing additional troops and creating a naval blockade of Yorktown. He was transporting 500,000 silver pesos collected from the citizens of Havana, Cuba, to fund supplies for the siege and payroll for the Continental Army. While in Santo Domingo, de Grasse met with Francisco Saavedra de Sangronis, an agent of Carlos III of Spain. De Grasse had planned to leave several of his warships in Santo Domingo. Saavedra promised the assistance of the Spanish navy to protect the French merchant fleet, enabling de Grasse to sail north with all of his warships. In the beginning of September, he defeated a British fleet led by Sir Thomas Graves that came to relieve Cornwallis at the Battle of the Chesapeake. As a result of this victory, de Grasse blocked any escape by sea for Cornwallis. By late September Washington and Rochambeau arrived, and the army and naval forces completely surrounded Cornwallis.

After initial preparations, the Americans and French built their first parallel and began the bombardment. With the British defense weakened, on October 14, 1781 Washington sent two columns to attack the last major remaining British outer defenses. A French column under Wilhelm of the Palatinate-Zweibrücken took Redoubt No. 9 and an American column under Alexander Hamilton took Redoubt No. 10. With these defenses taken, the allies were able to finish their second parallel. With the American artillery closer and its bombardment more intense than ever, the British position began to deteriorate rapidly and Cornwallis asked for capitulation terms on October 17. After two days of negotiation, the surrender ceremony occurred on October 19; Lord Cornwallis was absent from the ceremony. With the capture of more than 7,000 British soldiers, negotiations between the United States and Great Britain began, resulting in the Treaty of Paris of 1783.

History of the Yorktown Campaign

The Yorktown or Virginia campaign was a series of military maneuvers and battles during the American Revolutionary War that culminated in the decisive Siege of Yorktown in October 1781. The result of the campaign was the surrender of the British Army force of General Charles Earl Cornwallis, an event that led directly to the beginning of serious peace negotiations and the eventual end of the war. The campaign was marked by disagreements, indecision, and miscommunication on the part of British leaders, and by a remarkable set of cooperative decisions, at times in violation of orders, by the French and Americans.

The campaign involved land and naval forces of Great Britain and France, and land forces of the United States. British forces were sent to Virginia between January and April 1781 and joined with Cornwallis's army in May, which came north from an extended campaign through the southern states. These forces were first opposed weakly by Virginia militia, but General George Washington sent first Marquis de Lafayette and then Anthony Wayne with Continental Army troops to oppose the raiding and economic havoc the British were wreaking. The combined American forces, however, were insufficient in number to oppose the combined British forces, and it was only after a series of controversially confusing orders by General Sir Henry Clinton, the British commander-in-chief, that Cornwallis moved to Yorktown in July and built a defensive position that was strong against the land forces he then faced, but was vulnerable to naval blockade and siege.

British naval forces in North America and the West Indies were weaker than the combined fleets of France and Spain, and, after some critical decisions and tactical missteps by British naval commanders, the French fleet of Paul de Grasse gained control over Chesapeake Bay, blockading Cornwallis from naval support and delivering additional land forces to blockade him on land. The Royal Navy attempted to dispute this control, but Admiral Thomas Graves was defeated in the key Battle of the Chesapeake on September 5. American and French armies that had massed outside New York

City began moving south in late August, and arrived near Yorktown in mid-September. Deceptions about their movement successfully delayed attempts by Clinton to send more troops to Cornwallis.

The Siege of Yorktown began on September 28, 1781. In a step that probably shortened the siege, Cornwallis decided to abandon parts of his outer defenses, and the besiegers successfully stormed two of his redoubts. When it became clear that his position was untenable, Cornwallis opened negotiations on October 17 and surrendered two days later. When the news reached London, the government of Lord North fell, and the following Rockingham ministry entered into peace negotiations. These culminated in the Treaty of Paris in 1783, in which King George III recognized the independent United States of America. Clinton and Cornwallis engaged in a public war of words defending their roles in the campaign, and British naval command also discussed the navy's shortcomings that led to the defeat.

By December 1780, the American Revolutionary War's North American theaters had reached a critical point. The Continental Army had suffered major defeats earlier in the year, with its southern armies either captured or dispersed in the loss of Charleston and the Battle of Camden in the south, while the armies of George Washington and the British commander-in-chief for North America, Sir Henry Clinton watched each other around New York City in the north. The national currency was virtually worthless, public support for the war, about to enter its sixth year, was waning, and army troops were becoming mutinous over pay and conditions. In the Americans' favor, Loyalist recruiting in the south had been checked with a severe blow at Kings Mountain in October.

By December 1780, the American Revolutionary War's North American theaters had reached a critical point. The Continental Army had suffered major defeats earlier in the year, with its southern armies either captured or dispersed in the loss of Charleston and the Battle of Camden in the south, while the armies of George Washington and the British commander-in-chief for North America, Sir Henry Clinton watched each other around New York City in the north. The national currency was virtually worthless, public support for the war, about to enter its sixth year, was waning, and army troops were becoming mutinous over pay and conditions. In the Americans' favor, Loyalist recruiting in the south had been checked with a severe blow at Kings Mountain in October.

French and American planning for 1781

Virginia had largely escaped military notice before 1779, when a raid destroyed much of the state's shipbuilding capacity and seized or destroyed large amounts of tobacco, which was a significant trade item for the Americans. Virginia's only defenses consisted of locally raised militia companies, and a naval force that had been virtually wiped out in the 1779 raid. The militia were under the overall direction of Continental Army General Baron von Steuben, a prickly Prussian taskmaster who, although he was an excellent drillmaster, alienated not only his subordinates, but also had a difficult relationship with the state's governor, Thomas Jefferson. Steuben had established a training center in Chesterfield for new Continental Army recruits, and a "factory" in Westham for the manufacture and repair of weapons and ammunition.

French military planners had to balance competing demands for the 1781 campaign. After a series of unsuccessful attempts at cooperation with the Americans (leading to failed assaults on Newport, Rhode Island and Savannah, Georgia), they realized more active participation in North America was needed. However, they also needed to coordinate their actions with Spain, where there was potential interest in making an assault on the British stronghold of Jamaica. It turned out that the Spanish were not interested in operations against Jamaica until after they had dealt with an expected British attempt to reinforce besieged Gibraltar, and merely wanted to be informed of the movements of the West Indies fleet.

As the French fleet was preparing to depart Brest in March 1781, several important decisions were made. The West Indies fleet, led by the Comte de Grasse, after operations in the Windward Islands, was directed to go to Cap-Français (present-day Cap-Haïtien) to determine what resources would be required to assist Spanish operations. Due to a lack of transports, France also promised six million livres to support the American war effort instead of providing additional troops. The French fleet at Newport was given a new commander, the Comte de Barras. De Barras was ordered to take the Newport fleet to harass British shipping off Nova Scotia and Newfoundland, and the French army at Newport was ordered to combine with Washington's army outside New York. In orders that were deliberately not fully shared with General Washington, De Grasse was instructed to assist in North American operations after his stop at Cap-Français. The French general, the Comte de Rochambeau was instructed to tell Washington that de Grasse might be able to assist, without making any commitment. (Washington learned from John Laurens, stationed in Paris, that de Grasse had discretion to come north.)

The French fleet sailed from Brest on March 22. The British fleet was busy with preparations to resupply Gibraltar, and did not attempt to oppose the departure. After the French fleet sailed, the packet ship Concorde sailed for Newport, carrying the Comte de Barras, Rochambeau's orders, and credits for the six million livres. In a separate dispatch sent later, de Grasse also made two important requests. The first was that he be notified at Cap-Français of the situation in North America so that he could decide how he might be able to assist in operations there, and the second was that he be supplied with 30 pilots familiar with North American waters.

British planning for 1781

General Clinton never articulated a coherent vision for what the goals for British operations of the coming campaign season should be in the early months of 1781. Part of his problem lay in a difficult relationship with his naval counterpart in New York, the aging Vice Admiral Marriot Arbuthnot. Both men were stubborn, prone to temper, and had prickly personalities; due to repeated clashes, their working relationship had completely broken down. In the fall of 1780 Clinton had requested that either he or Arbuthnot be recalled; however, orders recalling Arbuthnot did not arrive until June 1781.

Until then, according to historian George Billias, "The two men could not act alone, and would not act together". Arbuthnot was replaced by Sir Thomas Graves, with whom Clinton had a somewhat better working relationship.

The British presence in the south consisted of the strongly fortified ports of Savannah, Georgia and Charleston, South Carolina, and a string of outposts in the interior of those two states. Although the strongest outposts were relatively immune to attack from the Patriot militia that were their only formal opposition in those states, the smaller outposts, as well as supply convoys and messengers, were often the target of militia commanders like Thomas Sumter and Francis Marion. Portsmouth had most recently been occupied in October 1780 by a force under the command of Major General Alexander Leslie, but Lieutenant General Charles, Earl Cornwallis, commanding the British southern army, had ordered them to South Carolina in November. To replace General Leslie at Portsmouth, General Clinton sent 1,600 troops under General Benedict Arnold (recently commissioned into the British Army as a brigadier) to Virginia in late December.

British raiding in Virginia

Part of the fleet carrying General Arnold and his troops arrived in Chesapeake Bay on December 30, 1780. Without waiting for the rest of the transports to arrive, Arnold sailed up the James River and disembarked 900 troops at Westover, Virginia, on January 4. After an overnight forced march, he raided Richmond, the state capital, the next day, encountering only minimal militia resistance. After two more days of raiding in the area, they returned to their boats, and made sail for Portsmouth. Arnold established fortifications there, and sent his men out on raiding and foraging expeditions. The local militia were called out, but they were in such small numbers that the British presence could not be disputed. This did not prevent raiding expeditions from running into opposition, as some did in skirmishing at Waters Creek in March.

Benedict Arnold

When news of Arnold's activities reached George Washington, he decided that a response was necessary. He wanted the French to send a naval expedition from their base in Newport, but the commanding admiral, Chevalier Destouches, refused any assistance until he received reports of serious storm damage to part of the

British fleet on January 22. On February 9, Captain Arnaud de Gardeur de Tilley sailed from Newport with three ships (ship of the line Eveille and frigates Surveillante and Gentile). When he arrived off Portsmouth four days later, Arnold withdrew his ships, which had shallower drafts than those of the French, up the Elizabeth River, where de Tilley could not follow. De Tilley, after determining that the local militia were "completely insufficient" to attack Arnold's position, returned to Newport. On the way he captured the HMS Romulus, a frigate sent by the British from New York to investigate his movements.

Congress authorized a detachment of Continental forces to Virginia on February 20. Washington assigned command of the expedition to the Marquis de Lafayette, who left Peekskill, New York the same day. His troops, numbering about 1,200, were three light regiments drawn from troops assigned to Continental regiments from New Jersey and New England; these regiments were led by Joseph Vose, Francis Barber, and Jean-Joseph Sourbader de Gimat. Lafayette's force reached Head of Elk (present-day Elkton, Maryland, the northern navigable limit of Chesapeake Bay) on March 3. While awaiting transportation for his troops at Annapolis, Lafayette traveled south, reaching Yorktown on March 14, to assess the situation.

The Marquis de Lafayette

American attempts at defense

De Tilley's expedition, and the strong encouragement of General Washington, who traveled to Newport to press the case, convinced Destouches to make a larger commitment. On March 8 he sailed with his entire fleet (7 ships of the line and several frigates, including the recently captured Romulus), carrying French troops to join with Lafayette's in Virginia. Admiral Arbuthnot, alerted to his departure, sailed on March 10 after sending Arnold a dispatch warning of the French movement. Arbuthnot, whose copper-clad ships could sail faster than those of Destouches, reached Cape Henry on March 16, just ahead of the French fleet. The ensuing battle was largely indecisive, but left Arbuthnot free to enter Lynnhaven Bay and control access to Chesapeake Bay; Destouches returned to Newport. Lafayette saw the British fleet, and pursuant to orders, made preparations to return his troops to the New York area. By early April he had returned to Head of Elk, where he received orders from Washington to stay in Virginia.

The departure of Destouches' fleet from Newport had prompted General Clinton to send Arnold reinforcements. In the wake of Arbuthnot's sailing he sent transports carrying about 2,000 men under the command of General William Phillips to the Chesapeake. These joined Arnold at Portsmouth on March 27. Phillips, as senior commander, took over the force and resumed raiding, targeting Petersburg and Richmond. By this time, Baron von Steuben and Peter Muhlenberg, the militia commanders in Virginia, felt they had to make a stand to maintain morale despite the inferior strength of their troops. They established a defensive line in Blandford, near Petersburg (Blandford is now a part of the city of Petersburg), and fought a disciplined but losing action on April 25. Von Steuben and Muhlenberg retreated before the advance of Phillips, who hoped to again raid Richmond. However, Lafayette made a series of forced marches, and reached Richmond on April 29, just hours before Phillips.

Admiral Marriot Arbuthnot

Cornwallis and Lafayette

To counter the British threat in the Carolinas, Washington had sent Major General Nathanael Greene, one of his best strategists, to rebuild the American army in North Carolina after the defeat at

General Charles, Earl Cornwallis

Camden. General Cornwallis, leading the British troops in the south, wanted to deal with him and gain control over the state. Greene divided his inferior force, sending part of his army under Daniel Morgan to threaten the British post at Ninety Six, South Carolina. Cornwallis sent Banastre Tarleton after Morgan, who almost wiped out Tarleton's command in the January 1781 Battle of Cowpens, and almost captured Tarleton in the process. This action was followed by what has been called the "race to the Dan," in which Cornwallis gave chase to Morgan and Greene in an attempt to catch them before they reunited their forces. When Greene successfully crossed the Dan River and entered Virginia, Cornwallis, who had stripped his army of most of its baggage, gave up the pursuit. However, Greene received reinforcements and supplies, recrossed the Dan, and returned to Greensboro, North Carolina to do battle with Cornwallis. The earl won the battle, but Greene was able to withdraw with his army intact, and the British suffered enough casualties that Cornwallis was forced to retreat to Wilmington for reinforcement and resupply. Greene then went on to regain control over most of South Carolina and Georgia. Cornwallis, in violation of orders but also in the absence of significant strategic direction by General Clinton, decided to take his army, now numbering just 1,400 men, into Virginia on April 25; it was the same day that Phillips and von Steuben fought at Blandford.

Phillips, after Lafayette beat him to Richmond, turned back east, continuing to destroy military and economic targets in the area. On May 7, Phillips received a dispatch from Cornwallis, ordering him to Petersburg to effect a junction of their forces; three days later, Phillips arrived in Petersburg. Lafayette briefly cannonaded the British position there, but did not feel strong enough to actually make an attack. On May 13, Phillips died of a fever, and Arnold retook control of the force. This caused some grumbling amongst the men, since Arnold was not particularly well respected. While waiting for Cornwallis, the forces of Arnold and Lafayette watched each other. Arnold attempted to open communications with the marquis (who had orders from Washington to summarily hang Arnold), but the marquis returned his letters unopened. Cornwallis arrived in Petersburg on May 19, prompting Lafayette, who commanded under 1,000 Continentals and about 2,000 militia, to retreat to Richmond. Further British reinforcements led by the Ansbacher Colonel von Voigt arrived from New York shortly after, raising the size of Cornwallis's army to more than 7,000.

Cornwallis, after dispatching General Arnold back to New York, then set out to follow General Clinton's most recent orders to Phillips. These instructions were to establish a fortified base and raid rebel military and economic targets in Virginia. Cornwallis decided that he had to first deal with the threat posed by Lafayette, so he set out in pursuit of the marquis. Lafayette, clearly outnumbered, retreated rapidly toward Fredericksburg to protect an important supply depot there, while von Steuben retreated to Point of Fork (present-day Columbia, Virginia), where militia and Continental Army trainees had gathered with supplies pulled back before the raiding British. Cornwallis reached the Hanover County courthouse on June 1, and, rather than send his whole army after Lafayette, detached Banastre Tarleton and John Graves Simcoe on separate raiding expeditions.

Tarleton, his British Legion reduced by the debacle at Cowpens, rode rapidly with a small force to Charlottesville, where he captured several members of the Virginia legislature. He almost captured Governor Jefferson as well, but had to content himself with several bottles of wine from Jefferson's estate at Monticello. Simcoe went to Point of Fork to deal with von Steuben and the supply depot. In a brief skirmish on June 5, von Steuben's forces, numbering about 1,000, suffered 30 casualties, but they had withdrawn most of the supplies across the river. Simcoe, who only had about 300 men, then exaggerated the size of his force by lighting a large number of campfires; this prompted von Steuben to withdraw from Point of Fork, leaving the supplies to be destroyed by Simcoe the next day.

Lafayette, in the meantime, was expecting the imminent arrival of long-delayed reinforcements. Several battalions of Pennsylvania Continentals under Brigadier General Anthony Wayne had also been authorized by Congress for service in Virginia in February. However, Wayne had to deal with the aftereffects of a mutiny in January that nearly wiped out the Pennsylvania Line as a fighting force, and it was May before he had rebuilt the line and begun the march to Virginia. Even then, there was a great deal of mistrust between Wayne and his men; Wayne had to keep his ammunition and bayonets under lock and key except when they were needed. Although Wayne was ready to march on May 19, the force's departure was delayed by a day because of a renewed threat of mutiny after the units were paid with devalued Continental dollars. Lafayette and Wayne's 800 men joined forces at Raccoon Ford on the Rappahannock River on June 10. A few days later, Lafayette was further reinforced by 1,000 militia under the command of William Campbell.

After the successful raids of Simcoe and Tarleton, Cornwallis began to make his way east toward Richmond and Williamsburg, almost contemptuously ignoring Lafayette in his movements. Lafayette, his force grown to about 4,500, was buoyed in confidence, and began to edge closer to the earl's army. By the time Cornwallis reached Williamsburg on June 25, Lafayette was 10 miles (16 km) away, at Bird's Tavern. That day, Lafayette learned that Simcoe's Queen's Rangers were at some remove from the main British force, so Lafayette sent some cavalry and light infantry to intercept them. This precipitated a skirmish at Spencer's Ordinary where each side believed the other to be within range of its main army.

Allied decisions

While Lafayette, Arnold, and Phillips maneuvered in Virginia, the allied leaders, Washington and Rochambeau, considered their options. On May 6 the Concorde arrived in Boston, and two days later Washington and Rochambeau were informed of the arrival of de Barras as well as the vital dispatches and funding. On May 23 and 24, Washington and Rochambeau held a conference at Wethersfield, Connecticut where they discussed what steps to take next. They agreed that, pursuant to his orders, Rochambeau would move his army from Newport to the Continental Army camp at White Plains, New York. They also decided to send dispatches to de Grasse outlining two possible courses of action. Washington favored the idea of attacking New York, while Rochambeau favored action in Virginia, where the British were less well established. Washington's letter to de Grasse outlined these two options; Rochambeau, in a private note, informed de Grasse of his preference. Lastly, Rochambeau convinced de Barras to hold his fleet in readiness to assist in either operation, rather than taking it out on expeditions to the north as he had been ordered. The Concorde sailed from Newport on June 20, carrying dispatches from Washington, Rochambeau, and de Barras, as well as the pilots de Grasse had requested. The French army left Newport in June, and joined Washington's army at Dobb's Ferry, New York on July 7. From there, Washington and Rochambeau embarked on an inspection tour of the British defenses around New York while they awaited word from de Grasse.

Lieutenant Colonel John Graves Simcoe

De Grasse had a somewhat successful campaign in the West Indies. His forces successfully captured Tobago in June after a minor engagement with the British fleet. Beyond that, he and British

Admiral George Brydges Rodney avoided significant engagement. De Grasse arrived at Cap-Français on July 16, where the Concorde awaited him. He immediately engaged in negotiations with the Spanish. He informed them of his intent to sail north, but promised to return by November to assist in Spanish operations in exchange for critical Spanish cover while he sailed north. From them he secured the promise to protect French commerce and territories so that he could bring north his entire fleet, 28 ships of the line. In addition to his fleet, he took on 3,500 troops under the command of the Marquis de St. Simon, and appealed to the Spanish in Havana for funds needed to pay Rochambeau's troops. On July 28, he sent the Concorde back to Newport, informing Washington, Rochambeau, and de Barras that he expected to arrive in the Chesapeake at the end of August, and would need to leave by mid-October. He sailed from Cap-Français on August 5, beginning a deliberately slow route north through a little-used channel in the Bahamas.

British decisions

The movement of the French army to the New York area caused General Clinton a great deal of concern; letters written by Washington that Clinton had intercepted suggested that the allies were planning an attack on New York. Beginning in June he wrote a series of letters to Cornwallis containing a confusing and controversial set of ruminations, suggestions, and recommendations, that only sometimes contained concrete and direct orders. Some of these letters were significantly delayed in reaching Cornwallis, complicating the exchange between the two. On June 11 and 15, apparently in reaction to the threat to New York, Clinton requested Cornwallis to fortify either Yorktown or Williamsburg, and send any troops he could spare back to New York. Cornwallis received these letters at Williamsburg on June 26. He and an engineer inspected Yorktown, which he found to be defensively inadequate. He wrote a letter to Clinton indicating that he would move to Portsmouth in order to send troops north with transports available there.

On July 4 Cornwallis began moving his army toward the Jamestown ferry, to cross the broad James River and march to Portsmouth. Lafayette's scouts observed the motion, and he realized the British force would be vulnerable during the crossing. He advanced his army to the Green Spring Plantation, and, based on intelligence that only the British rear guard was left at the crossing, sent General Wayne forward to attack them on July 6. In reality, the earl had laid a clever trap. Crossing only his baggage and some troops to guard them, he sent "deserters" to falsely inform Lafayette of the situation. In the Battle of Green Spring, General Wayne managed to escape the trap, but with significant casualties and the loss of two field pieces. Cornwallis then crossed the river, and marched his army to Suffolk.

Cornwallis again detached Tarleton on a raid into central Virginia. Tarleton's raid was based on intelligence that supplies might be intercepted that were en route to General Greene. The raid, in which Tarleton's force rode 120 miles (190 km) in four days, was a failure, since supplies had already been moved. (During this raid, some of Tarleton's men were supposedly in a minor skirmish with Peter Francisco, one of the American heroes of Guilford Court House.) Cornwallis received another letter from General Clinton while at Suffolk, dated June 20, stating that the forces to be embarked were to be used for an attack against Philadelphia.

When Cornwallis reached Portsmouth, he began embarking troops pursuant to Clinton's orders. On July 20, with some transports almost ready to sail, new orders arrived that countermanded the previous ones. In the most direct terms, Clinton ordered him to establish a fortified deep-water port, using as much of his army as he thought necessary. Clinton took this decision because the navy had long been dissatisfied with New York as a naval base, firstly because sand bars obstructed the entrance to the Hudson River, damaging the hulls of the larger ships; and secondly because the river often froze in winter, imprisoning vessels inside the harbour. Arbuthnot had recently been replaced and to show his satisfaction at this development, Clinton now acceded to the Navy's request, despite Cornwallis's warning that the Chesapeake's open bays and navigable rivers meant that any base there "will always be exposed to sudden French attack." It was to prove a fatal error of judgement by Clinton, since the need to defend the new facility denied Cornwallis any freedom of movement . Nevertheless, having inspected Portsmouth and found it less favourable than Yorktown, Cornwallis wrote to Clinton informing him that he would fortify Yorktown.

Lafayette was alerted on July 26 that Cornwallis was embarking his troops, but lacked intelligence about their eventual destination, and began maneuvering his troops to cover some possible landing points. On August 6 he learned that Cornwallis had landed at Yorktown and was fortifying it and Gloucester Point just across the York River.

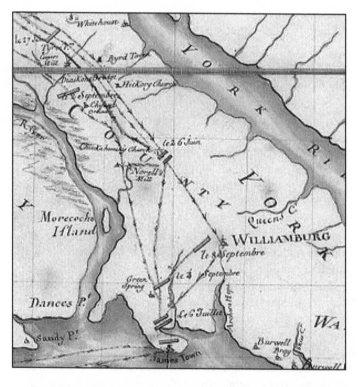

Detail from a 1781 French map prepared for Lafayette depicting the Williamsburg/Jamestown area and the movements of Lafayette and Cornwallis. The clash at Spencer's is marked by "le 26 Juin", and that at Green Spring is labelled "le 6 Juillet".

Convergence on Yorktown

Admiral Rodney had been warned that de Grasse was planning to take at least part of his fleet north. Although he had some clues that he might take his whole fleet (he was aware of the number of pilots de Grasse had requested, for example), he assumed that de Grasse would not leave the French convoy at Cap-Français, and that part of his fleet would escort it to France as Admiral Guichen had done the previous year. Rodney made his dispositions accordingly, balancing the likely requirements of the fleet in North America with the need to protect Britain's own trade convoys. Sixteen of his twenty-one battleships, therefore, were to sail with Hood in pursuit of de Grasse to the Chesapeake before proceeding to New York. Rodney, who was ill, meanwhile took three other battleships back to England, two as merchant escorts, leaving his remaining two in dock for repairs. Hood was well satisfied with these arrangements, telling a colleague that his fleet was "equal fully to defeat any designs of the enemy, let de Grasse bring or send what number of ships he might in aid of Barras." What neither Rodney or Hood knew was de Grasse's last minute decision to take his entire fleet to North America, thus ensuring a French superiority of three to two in battleship strength. Blissfully unaware of this development, Hood eventually sailed from Antigua on August 10, five days after de Grasse. During the voyage, one of his smaller ships carrying intelligence about the American pilots was captured by a privateer, thus further depriving the British in New York of valuable information. Hood himself, following the direct route, reached the Chesapeake on August 25, and found the entrance to the bay empty. He then sailed on to New York to meet with Admiral Sir Thomas Graves, in command of the New York station following Arbuthnot's departure.

On August 14 General Washington learned of de Grasse's decision to sail for the Chesapeake. The next day he reluctantly abandoned the idea of assaulting New York, writing that "matters having now come to a crisis and a decisive plan to be determined on, I was obliged ... to give up all idea of attacking New York..." The combined Franco-American army began moving south on August 19, engaging in several tactics designed to fool Clinton about their intentions. Some forces were sent on a route along the New Jersey shore, and ordered to make camp preparations as if preparing for an attack on Staten Island. The army also carried landing craft to lend verisimilitude to the idea. Washington sent orders to Lafayette to prevent Cornwallis from returning to North Carolina; he did not learn that Cornwallis was entrenching at Yorktown until August 30. Two days later the army was passing through Philadelphia; another mutiny was averted there when funds were procured for troops that threatened to stay until they were paid.

Admiral de Barras sailed with his fleet from Newport, carrying the French siege equipment, on August 25. He sailed a route that deliberately took him away from the coast to avoid encounters with the British. De Grasse reached the Chesapeake on August 30, five days after Hood. He immediately debarked the troops from his fleet to assist Lafayette in blockading Cornwallis, and stationed some his ships to blockade the York and James Rivers.

News of de Barras' sailing reached New York on August 28, where Graves, Clinton, and Hood were meeting to discuss the possibility of making an attack on the French fleet in Newport, since the French army was no longer there to defend it. Clinton had still not realized that Washington was marching south, something he did not have confirmed until September 2. When they learned of de Barras' departure they immediately concluded that de Grasse must be headed for the Chesapeake (but still did not know of his strength). Graves sailed from New York on August 31 with 19 ships of the line; Clinton wrote Cornwallis to warn him that Washington was coming, and that he would send 4,000 reinforcements.

On September 5, the British fleet arrived at the mouth of the Chesapeake to see the French fleet anchored there. De Grasse, who had men ashore, was forced to cut his cables and scramble to get his fleet out to meet the British. In the Battle of the Chesapeake, de Grasse won a narrow tactical victory. After the battle, the two fleets drifted to the southeast for several days, with the British avoiding battle and both fleets making repairs. This was apparently in part a ploy by de Grasse to ensure the British would not interfere with de

Barras' arrival. A fleet was spotted off in the distance on September 9 making for the bay; de Grasse followed the next day. Graves, forced to scuttle one of his ships, returned to New York for repairs. Smaller ships from the French fleet then assisted in transporting the Franco-American army down the Chesapeake to Yorktown, completing the encirclement of Cornwallis.

The Siege

On September 26, transports with artillery, siege tools, and some French infantry and shock troops from Head of Elk, the northern end of the Chesapeake Bay, arrived, giving Washington command of an army of 7,800 Frenchmen, 3,100 militia, and 8,000 Continentals. Early on September 28, Washington led the army out of Williamsburg to surround Yorktown. The French took the positions on the left while the Americans took the position of honor on the right. Cornwallis had a chain of seven redoubts and batteries linked by earthworks along with batteries that covered the narrows of the York River at Gloucester Point. That day, Washington reconnoitered the British defenses and decided that they could be bombarded into submission. The Americans and the French spent the night of the 28th sleeping out in the open, while work parties built bridges over the marsh. Some of the American soldiers hunted down wild hogs to eat.

On September 29, Washington moved the army closer to Yorktown and British gunners opened fire on the infantry. Throughout the day several British cannon fired on the Americans but there were few casualties. Fire was also exchanged between American riflemen and Hessian Jägers.

Cornwallis pulled back from all of his outer defenses, except for the Fusilier's redoubt on the west side of the town and redoubts 9 and 10 in the east. Cornwallis had his forces occupy the earthworks immediately surrounding the town because he had received a letter from Clinton that promised relief force of 5,000 men within a week and he wished to tighten his lines. The Americans and the French occupied the abandoned defenses and began to establish their own batteries there. With the British outer defenses in their hands, allied engineers began to lay out positions for the artillery. The men improved their works and deepened their trenches. The British also worked on improving their defenses.

On September 30, the French attacked the British Fusiliers redoubt. The skirmish lasted two hours, in which the French were repulsed suffering several casualties. On October 1, the allies learned from British deserters that, to preserve their food, the British had slaughtered hundreds of horses and thrown them on the beach. In the American camp, thousands of trees were cut down to provide wood for earthworks. Preparations for the parallel also began.

As the allies began to put their artillery into place, the British kept up a steady fire to disrupt them. British fire increased on the 2nd and the allies suffered moderate casualties. General Washington continued to make visits to the front, despite concern shown by several of his officers over the increasing enemy fire. On the night of October 2, the British opened a storm of fire to cover up the movement of the British cavalry to Gloucester where they were to escort infantrymen on a foraging party. On the 3rd, the foraging party, led by Banastre Tarleton, went out but collided with Lauzun's Legion, and John Mercer's Virginia militia, led by the Marquis de Choisy. The British cavalry quickly retreated back behind their defensive lines, losing 50 men.

By October 5, Washington was almost ready to open the first parallel. That night the sappers and miners worked, putting strips of pine on the wet sand to mark the path of the trenches.

Bombardment

After nightfall on October 6, troops moved out in stormy weather to dig the first parallel: the heavily overcast sky negated the waning full moon and shielded the massive digging operation from the eyes of British sentries. Washington ceremoniously struck several blows with his pick axe to begin the trench. The trench was to be 2,000 yards (1,800 m) long, running from the head of Yorktown to the York River. Half of the trench was to be commanded by the French, the other half by the Americans. On the northernmost end of the French line, a support trench was dug so that they could bombard the British ships in the river. The French were ordered to distract the British with a false attack, but the British were told of the plan by a French deserter and the British artillery fire turned on the French from the Fusiliers redoubt.

On October 7, the British saw the new allied trench just out of musket-range. Over the next two days the allies completed the gun placements and dragged the artillery into line. The British fire began to weaken when they saw the large number of guns the allies had.

By October 9, all of the French and American guns were in place. Among the American guns there were three twenty-four pounders, three eighteen pounders, two eight-inch (203 mm) howitzers and six mortars, totaling fourteen guns. At 3:00 pm, the French guns opened the barrage and drove the British frigate, HMS Guadeloupe across the York River, where she was scuttled to prevent capture. At 5:00 pm the Americans opened fire. Washington fired the first gun; legend has it that this shot smashed into a table where British officers were eating. The Franco-American guns began to tear apart the British defenses. Washington ordered that the guns fire all night so that the British could not make repairs. All of the British guns on the left were soon silenced. The British soldiers began to pitch their tents in their trenches and soldiers began to desert in large numbers. Some British ships were also damaged by cannonballs that flew across the town into the harbor.

On October 10, the Americans spotted a large house in Yorktown. Believing that Cornwallis might be stationed there, they aimed at it and quickly destroyed it. Cornwallis sank more than a dozen of his ships in the harbor. The French began to fire at the British ships and scored a hit on the British HMS Charon, which caught fire, and in turn set two or three other ships on fire. Cornwallis received word from Clinton that the British fleet was to depart on October 12, however Cornwallis responded by saying that he would not be able to hold out for long.

On the night of October 11, Washington ordered that the Americans dig a second parallel. It was 400 yards (370 m) closer to the British lines, but could not be extended to the river because the British number 9 and 10 redoubts were in the way. During the night, the British fire continued to land in the old line; Cornwallis did not suspect that a new parallel was being dug. By morning of the 12th, the allied troops were in position on the new line.

By October 14, the trenches were within 150 yards (140 m) of redoubts No. 9 and No. 10. Washington ordered that all guns within range begin blasting the redoubts to weaken them for an assault that evening. Washington planned to use the cover of a moonless night to gain the element of surprise. To reinforce the darkness, he added silence, ordering that no soldier should load his musket until reaching the fortifications- the advance would be made with only "cold steel." Redoubt 10 was near the river and held only 70 men, while redoubt 9 was a quarter of a mile inland, and was held by 120 British and Germans. Both redoubts were heavily fortified with rows of abatis surrounding them, along with muddy ditches that surrounded the redoubts at about 25 yards (23 m). Washington devised a plan in which the French would launch a diversionary attack on the Fusiliers redoubt, and then a half an hour later, the French would assault redoubt 9 and the Americans redoubt 10. Redoubt 9 would be assaulted by 400 French regular soldiers under the command of the German Lieutenant Colonel Wilhelm von Zweibrücken and redoubt 10 would be assaulted by 400 light infantry troops under the command of Alexander Hamilton. There was briefly a dispute as to who should lead the attack on Redoubt No. 10. Lafayette named his aide, Jean-Joseph Sourbader de Gimat, who commanded a battalion of Continental light infantry. However, Hamilton protested, saying that he was the senior officer. Washington concurred with Hamilton and gave him command of the attack.

At 6:30 pm, gunfire announced the diversionary attack on the Fusiliers redoubt. At other places in the line, movements were made as if preparing for an assault on Yorktown itself, which caused the British to panic. With bayonets fixed, the Americans marched towards Redoubt No. 10. Hamilton sent Lieutenant Colonel John Laurens around to the rear of the redoubt to prevent the British from escaping. The Americans reached the redoubt and began chopping through the British wooden defenses with their axes. A British sentry called a challenge, and then fired at the Americans. The Americans responded by charging with their bayonets towards the redoubt. They hacked through the abatis, crossed a ditch and climbed the parapet into the redoubt. The Americans forced their way into the redoubt falling into giant shell holes from the bombardment of the redoubts. The British fire was heavy, but the Americans overwhelmed them. Someone in the front shouted, "Rush on boys! The fort's ours!" The British threw hand grenades at the Americans with little effect. Men in the trench stood on the shoulders of their comrades to climb into the redoubt. The bayonet fight cleared the British out of the redoubt and almost the entire garrison was captured, including the commander of the redoubt, Major Campbell. In the assault, the Americans lost 9 dead and 25 wounded.

The French assault began at the same time, but they were halted by the abatis, which was undamaged by the artillery fire. The French began to hack at the abatis and a Hessian sentry came out and asked who was there. When there was no response, the sentry opened fire as did other Hessians on the parapet. The French soldiers fired back, and then charged the redoubt. The Germans charged the Frenchmen climbing over the walls but the French fired a volley, driving them back. The Hessians then took a defensive position behind some barrels but threw down their arms and surrendered when the French prepared a bayonet charge.

With the capture of redoubts 9 and 10, Washington was able to have his artillery shell the town from three directions and the allies moved some of their artillery into the redoubts. On October 15, Cornwallis turned all of his guns onto the nearest allied position. He then ordered a storming party of 350 British troops under the command of Colonel Robert Abercromby to attack the allied lines and spike the American and French cannon (i.e., plug the touch hole with an iron spike). The allies were sleeping and unprepared. As the British charged Abercromby shouted "Push on my brave boys, and skin the bastards!" The British party spiked several cannon in the parallel and then spiked the guns on an unfinished redoubt. A French party came and drove them out of the allied lines and back to Yorktown. The British had been able to spike six guns, but by the morning they were all repaired. The bombardment resumed with the

American and French troops engaged in competition to see who could do the most damage to the enemy defenses.

On the morning of October 16, more allied guns were in line and the fire intensified. In desperation, Cornwallis attempted to evacuate his troops across the York River to Gloucester Point. At Gloucester Point the troops might be able to break through the allied lines and escape into Virginia and then march to New York. One wave of boats made it across but a squall hit when they returned to take more soldiers across, making the evacuation impossible.

British Surrender

The fire on Yorktown from the allies was heavier than ever as new artillery pieces joined the line. Cornwallis talked with his officers that day and they agreed that their situation was hopeless.

On the morning of October 17, a drummer appeared followed by an officer waving a white handkerchief. The bombardment ceased, and the officer was blindfolded and led behind the French and American lines. Negotiations began at the Moore House on October 18 between Lieutenant Colonel Thomas Dundas and Major Alexander Ross (who represented the British) and Lieutenant Colonel Laurens (who represented the Americans) and the Marquis de Noailles (who represented the French). To make sure that nothing fell apart between the French and Americans at the last minute, Washington ordered that the French be given an equal share in every step of the surrender process.

The articles of capitulation were signed on October 19, 1781. Signatories included Washington, Rochambeau, the Comte de Barras (on behalf of the French Navy), Cornwallis, and Captain Thomas Symonds (the senior Royal Navy officer present). Cornwallis' British men were declared prisoners of war, promised good treatment in American camps, and officers were permitted to return home after taking their parole. At 2:00 pm the allied army entered the British positions, with the French on the left and the Americans on the right.

The British had asked for the traditional honors of war, which would allow the army to march out with flags flying, bayonets fixed, and the band playing an American or French tune as a tribute to the victors. However, Washington firmly refused to grant the British the honors that they had denied the defeated American army the year before at the Siege of Charleston. Consequently, the British and Hessian troops marched with flags furled and muskets shouldered, while the band was forced to play "a British or German march." American history books recount the legend that the British band played "The World Turn'd Upside Down", but the story may be apocryphal.

Cornwallis refused to attend the surrender ceremony, citing illness. Instead, Brigadier General Charles O'Hara led the British army onto the field. O'Hara first attempted to surrender to Rochambeau, who shook his head and pointed to Washington. O'Hara then offered his sword to Washington, who also refused and motioned to Benjamin Lincoln. The surrender finally took place when Washington's second-in-command accepted the sword of Cornwallis' deputy.

The British soldiers marched out and laid down their arms in between the French and American armies, while many civilians watched. At this time, the troops on the other side of the river in Gloucester also surrendered. The British soldiers had been issued new uniforms hours before the surrender and until prevented by General O'Hara some threw down their muskets with the apparent intention of smashing them. Others wept or appeared to be drunk. In all, 8,000 troops, 214 artillery pieces, thousands of muskets, 24 transport ships, wagons and horses were captured.

Casualties

The French casualties were 60 killed and 194 wounded and the American casualties were 28 killed and 107 wounded: a grand total of 88 killed and 301 wounded.

The British official casualty return for the siege listed 156 killed, 326 wounded and 70 missing. Cornwallis surrendered 7,087 officers and enlisted men in Yorktown when he capitulated and a further 840 sailors from the British fleet in the York River. Another 84 prisoners had been taken during the assault on the redoubts on October 16. Since only 70 men were reported as missing, this would suggest that 14 of the men officially marked down as 'killed' had in fact been captured. This gives a grand total of 142 killed, 326 wounded prisoners and 7,685 other prisoners. Jerome A. Greene mentions a German account that gives much higher figures: 309 killed and 595 wounded.

Article 10 controversy

George Washington refused to accept the Tenth Article of the Yorktown Articles of Capitulation, which granted immunity to American Loyalists, and Cornwallis failed to make any effort to press the matter. "The outcry against the Tenth Article was vociferous and immediate, as Americans on both sides of the Atlantic proclaimed their sense of betrayal."

Effect of disease

Malaria was endemic in the marshlands of eastern Virginia during the time, and Cornwallis's army suffered greatly from the disease; he estimated during the surrender that half of his army was unable to fight as a result. The Continental Army enjoyed an advantage, in that most of their members had grown up with malaria, and hence had acquired resistance to the disease. As malaria has a month-long incubation period, most of the French soldiers had not begun to exhibit symptoms before the surrender.

Aftermath

The negotiations for surrender were complicated by two issues. When American forces surrendered at Charleston in 1780, they were not granted customary terms of capitulation that included flying colors and the playing of an enemy tune. Washington insisted that these terms be applied to the surrender of the British army at Yorktown, his negotiators pointing out that the defenders had in both instances acted with valor. The second issue concerned the disposition of Loyalists in the British camp. This issue was finessed with the addition of a clause to the terms that allowed one British vessel, the sloop Bonetta, to be sent without any sort of inspection to carry dispatches from Cornwallis to New York; Americans, suspecting that either runaway slaves or Loyalists might be aboard, were prevented from searching the vessel.

When the British garrison marched out of their positions on October 19 to surrender, it was with colors cased, possibly playing the British tune "The World Turned Upside Down". Cornwallis, claiming illness, did not attend the ceremony, sending his deputy General O'Hara to deliver his sword. O'Hara at first sought to deliver it to a French officer, but he was finally directed to one of Washington's officers, Benjamin Lincoln, the defeated commander at Charleston. Lincoln briefly held the proferred sword and then returned it to O'Hara.

Over the following weeks, the army was marched under guard to camps in Virginia and Maryland. Cornwallis and other officers were returned to New York and allowed to return to England on parole. The ship on which Cornwallis sailed in December 1781 also carried Benedict Arnold and his family.

Disposition of the allies

The local militia that supported the siege were dismissed from service. Some of the American Continental forces were returned to the New York City region, where Washington continued to stand against the British presence until the end of the war; others were sent south to assist in General Greene's efforts in the Carolinas. Issues of pay and condition were an ongoing problem until the war ended, but Washington fought no more battles.

The French forces that came with de Grasse were reembarked, and he sailed for the West Indies, with the fleet of de Barras, in early November. After recapturing a number of British-held targets there, de Grasse was preparing to join with the Spanish for an assault on Jamaica when Admiral Rodney defeated him in the April 1782 Battle of the Saintes, capturing him and his flagship. The forces of General Rochambeau wintered in Virginia, and marched back to Rhode Island the next summer.

Reactions

General Washington's aide, Lieutenant Tench Tilghman, was dispatched to deliver the news to Congress. Arriving in Philadelphia on October 22, he was two days behind the first notice of the surrender, which had been expressed from Baltimore ahead of him. The news electrified Congress and the populace. Church bells pealed, and the Liberty Bell was reportedly rung, actions that were repeated as the news traveled through the colonies. Some Congressmen introduced a resolution calling on General Washington to arrest and hang General Cornwallis; after "the debate continue'd several Day's", the resolution was voted down.

The news put British-occupied New York City into mourning. At first met with some skepticism, the news was finally confirmed on October 27, although the city still awaited news of Clinton's abortive relief effort. Clinton was recalled to London, and left the city in March 1782. He was replaced by General Guy Carleton, who was under orders to suspend offensive operations.

When the news reached London on November 25, Lord Germain described the reaction of Lord North to the news: "he would have taken a ball on his breast. For he opened his arms exclaiming wildly as he paced up and down the apartment, during the few minutes, 'Oh God! It is all over!'" King George was reported to receive the news with calmness and dignity, although he later became depressed as the news sank in, and even considered abdication. The king's supporters in Parliament were depressed, and the opposition elated. A resolution calling for an end to the war was introduced on December 12, and failed to pass by a single vote. Lord Germain was dismissed in early 1782, and the North administration fell shortly afterward. Peace negotiations followed, and the war was formally ended with the signing of the Treaty of Paris on September 3, 1783.

General Cornwallis, despite being the commander who surrendered, was not blamed for the defeat. He was well-received on his return to London, and one writer echoed a common sentiment that "Lord Cornwallis's army was sold." General Clinton spent the rest of his life defending his own reputation; he was "laughed at by the rebels, despised by the British, and cursed by the loyalists." In 1783, he published a Narrative of the Campaign of 1781 in North America in which he attempted to lay the blame for the 1781 campaign failures on General Cornwallis. This was met with a public response by Cornwallis, who leveled his own criticisms at Clinton. The highly public debate included the publication of much of their correspondence.

Admiral Graves also did not suffer due to his defeat by de Grasse; he was eventually promoted to full admiral and given a peerage. However, many aspects of the Battle of the Chesapeake have been the subject of both contemporary and historical debate, beginning right after the battle. On 6 September, Admiral Graves issued a memorandum justifying a confusing use of signals, indicating that "when the signal for the line of battle ahead is out at the same time with the signal for battle, it is not to be understood that the latter signal shall be rendered ineffectual by a too strict adherence to the former." Hood, in commentary written on the reverse of his copy, observed that this eliminated any possibility of engaging an enemy who was disordered, since it would require the British line to also be disordered. Instead, he maintained, "the British fleet should be as compact as possible, in order to take the critical moment of an advantage opening ..." Others criticise Hood because he "did not wholeheartedly aid his chief", and that a lesser officer "would have been court-martialled for not doing his utmost to engage the enemy."

The Comte de Rochambeau dispatched two messengers to deliver the news to Paris in a move that had unusual consequences in French military politics. The Duc de Lauzun and the Comte de Deux-Pontes, both of whom had distinguished themselves in the siege, were sent on separate ships to bring the news. Deux-Pontes was accompanied by a favorite of the French naval minister the Marquis de Castries, the Comte de Charlus, who Lauzun had urged Rochambeau to send in his stead for political reasons. King Louis XVI and his ministers received the news warmly, but Castries and the snubbed Charlus ensured that Lauzun and Rochambeau were denied or delayed in the receipt of rewards for the success. Deux-Pontes was rewarded with the Order of Saint Louis and command of a regiment.

Analysis

Historian John Pancake describes the later stages of the campaign as "British blundering" and that the "allied operations proceeded with clockwork precision." Naval historian Jonathan Dull has described de Grasse's 1781 naval campaign, which encompassed, in addition to Yorktown, successful contributions to the French capture of Tobago and the Spanish siege of Pensacola, as the "most perfectly executed naval campaign of the age of sail", and compared the string of French successes favorably with the British Annus Mirabilis of 1759. He also observes that a significant number of individual decisions, at times against orders or previous agreements, contributed to the success of the campaign:

- French ministers Montmorin and Vergennes convinced the French establishment that decisive action was needed in North America in order to end the war.

- The French naval minister Castries wrote orders for de Grasse that gave the latter sufficient flexibility to assist in the campaign.
- Spanish Louisiana Governor Bernardo de Gálvez released ships and troops to cover French territories while de Grasse sailed north with most of the French military establishment in the West Indies.
- Spanish Cuban colonial official Francisco Saavedra cooperated in the decision-making that enabled de Grasse's northward expedition.
- General Rochambeau and Chevalier Luzerne both urged de Grasse to decide on the Chesapeake.
- Admiral de Barras violated his orders to operate off Newfoundland, making possible the timely delivery of the French siege train to Yorktown.
- George Washington decided against an attack on New York and instead embarked on a risky march to Virginia.
- Admiral De Grasse agreed to overstay his planned time in the Chesapeake, understanding the importance of the undertaking there.

Of de Grasse's negotiations with the Spanish that secured the use of his fleet and his order to the economic fleet to remain in the West Indies, Royal Navy Captain Thomas White, in his 1830 analysis of the 1781 campaign, wrote that "the British government had sanctioned, or a British admiral had adopted such a measure, the one would have been turned out, and the other would have been hung: no wonder they succeeded and we failed."

Legacy

On October 19, 1881, an elaborate ceremony took place to honor the battle's centennial. U.S. naval vessels floated on Chesapeake Bay, and special markers highlighted where Washington and Lafayette's siege guns were placed. President Chester Arthur, sworn in only thirty days before, following James Garfield's death, made his first public speech as president. Also present were descendants of Lafayette, Rochambeau, de Grasse, and Steuben. To close the ceremony, Arthur gave an order to salute the British flag.

There is a belief that General Cornwallis's sword, surrendered by Charles O'Hara after the battle, is to this day on display at the White House. However, U.S. National Park Service historian Jerome Green, in his 2005 history of the siege, The Guns of Independence, concurs with the 1881 centennial account by Johnston, noting simply that when Brigadier General O'Hara presented the sword to Major General Lincoln, he held it for a moment and immediately returned it to O'Hara.

The siege of Yorktown is also known in some German historiographies as "die deutsche Schlacht" ("the German battle"), because Germans played significant roles in all three armies, accounting for roughly one third of all forces involved. According to one estimate more than 2,500 German soldiers served at Yorktown with each of the British and French armies, and more than 3,000 German-Americans were in Washington's army.

Four Army National Guard units (113th Inf, 116th Inf, 175th Inf and 198th Sig Bn) and one active Regular Army Field Artillery battalion (1–5th FA) are derived from American units that participated in the Battle of Yorktown. There are thirty current U.S. Army units with lineages that go back the colonial era.